Life in the
THIRTEEN COLONIES

Connecticut

Emily Lauren

children's press®
An imprint of
■SCHOLASTIC

Library of Congress Cataloging-in-Publication Data

Lauren, Emily.
  Connecticut / by Emily Lauren.
    p. cm. — (Life in the thirteen colonies)
  Includes bibliographical references and index.
  ISBN 0-516-24568-6
  1. Connecticut—History—Colonial period, ca. 1600–1775—Juvenile literature. 2. Connecticut—History—Revolution, 1775–1783—Juvenile literature. I. Title. II. Series.
  F97.L28 2004
  974.6'02—dc22

                              2004005029

3 4 5 6 7 8 9 10 R 13 12 11 10 09 08 07   62

A Creative Media Applications Production
Design: Fabia Wargin Design
Editor: Laura Walsh
Copy Editor: Laurie Lieb
Content Research: Lauren Thogersen
Photo Researcher: Annette Cyr
Content Consultant: David Silverman, Ph.D.

Photo credits © 2004
Cover: top left © Bettmann/CORBIS; top right © Getty Images/Hulton Archive; bottom left © North Wind Archives; bottom right © North Wind Archives; Background © North Wind Archives; title page © North Wind Archives; p. 2 © North Wind Archives; p. 4 © North Wind Archives; p. 7 © North Wind Archives; p. 9 © North Wind Archives; p. 12 © North Wind Archives; p. 22 © North Wind Archives; p. 25 © Getty Images/Hulton Archive; p. 26 © Getty Images/Hulton Archive; p. 28 © North Wind Archives; p. 33 © North Wind Archives; p. 34 © North Wind Archives; p. 39 © North Wind Archives; p. 41 © North Wind Archives; p. 42 © North Wind Archives; p. 47 © North Wind Archives; p. 49 © North Wind Archives; p. 50 © North Wind Archives; p. 53 © North Wind Archives; p. 55 © North Wind Archives; p. 58 © North Wind Archives; p. 63 © North Wind Archives; p. 64: top center © Colonial Williamsburg Foundation; bottom left © Getty Images/Hulton Archive; bottom center (arrow) © Geoffrey Clements/CORBIS; bottom center (arrowhead) © Andy Angstrom; center left © Getty Images/Hulton Archive; p. 65: top right (beaver) © Getty Images/Hulton Archive; top center (musket) © Colonial Williamsburg Foundation; center left © North Wind Archives; center right © Museum of the City of New York/CORBIS; center middle (beaver) © Tom Brakefield/CORBIS; bottom left © Getty Images/Hulton Archive; bottom right © Academy of Natural Sciences of Philadelphia/CORBIS; p. 66 © CORBIS; p. 69 © North Wind Archives; p. 72 © North Wind Archives; p. 77 © North Wind Archives; p. 78 © North Wind Archives; p. 81 © North Wind Archives; p. 84 © North Wind Archives; p. 86 © North Wind Archives; p. 88 © North Wind Archives; p. 90 © North Wind Archives; p. 93 © Getty Images/Hulton Archive; p. 95 © North Wind Archives; p. 102 © North Wind Archives; p. 104 © North Wind Archives; p. 106 © North Wind Archives; p. 108 © Getty Images/Hulton Archive; p. 110 © Getty Images/Hulton Archive; p. 112 © North Wind Archives; p. 115 © Getty Images/Hulton Archive; p. 117 © The Newbery Library; p. 118: top left © North Wind Archives; top right © North Wind Archives; bottom left © North Wind Archives; bottom right © North Wind Archives; p.119: top left © North Wind Archives; top right © North Wind Archives; bottom © North Wind Archives; background © North Wind Archives

CONTENTS

THE
ORIGINAL
THIRTEEN COLONIES,
1775

NEW FRANCE

MAINE
(part of Mass.)

St. Lawrence River

Lake Champlain

Lake Ontario

Mohawk R.

NEW HAMPSHIRE

• Falmouth

Portsmouth •
Newburyport •

Albany •

NEW YORK

Salem •
Boston •

MASSACHUSETTS

Cape Cod

Lake Erie

Hudson R.

Connecticut River

Hartford •

Newport •

New Haven •

RHODE ISLAND
CONNECTICUT

Delaware R.

Susquehanna R.

New York •

Long Island

Appalachian Mountains

PENNSYLVANIA

Perth Amboy •

Pittsburgh •

Philadelphia •

Burlington •

York •

New Castle •

NEW JERSEY

Baltimore •

Ohio River

Potomac R.

MARYLAND

DELAWARE

Alexandria •

Chesapeake Bay

James River

Richmond •

VIRGINIA

Williamsburg •

Norfolk •

Atlantic Ocean

Roanoke River

Edenton •

Hillsboro •

Halifax •

Salem •

NORTH CAROLINA

Bath •

Cape Hatteras

New Bern •

Salisbury •

Pamlico Sound

Charlotte •

Cross Creek •

Cape Fear R.

Camden •

Wilmington •

SOUTH CAROLINA

• Georgetown

Savannah River

Augusta •

GEORGIA

• Charles Town

Savannah •

NORTH

WEST

EAST

SOUTH

Legend

—— Colonial boundaries
(The western boundaries of many colonies were undefined in 1775.)

0   125   250

Scale in Miles

SPANISH TERRITORY

A Nation Grows From Thirteen Colonies

Connecticut lies in the northeastern region of the United States. It is bordered by Massachusetts to the north, New York on the west, and Rhode Island on the east. Its southern border is formed by Long Island Sound. Connecticut was discovered by accident when a Dutch explorer named Adriaen Block was stranded in America.

Before Europeans settled Connecticut, the region was home to many Native American tribes. They hunted and fished along the Connecticut River, Long Island Sound, and the dense forests that covered the area. The colony's **fertile** soil attracted Puritan farmers from Massachusetts Bay Colony. They came to Connecticut seeking religious freedom and a better life. The colony soon became a center of manufacturing. It was also important to the success of the Patriot cause during the American Revolution.

🖎 *The map shows the thirteen English colonies in 1775. The colored sections show the areas that were settled at that time.*

CHAPTER ONE

Long River Place

আআআআআআআআআআআআআআআআআআআআআআআআআআআআআআআআআআ

European Exploration

In 1613, a Dutchman named Adriaen Block set out on a ship called the *Tiger* to make his fortune. He would become the first European to set foot on the land that would someday become the state of Connecticut. Finding Connecticut was not Block's plan. He stumbled into the future colony quite by accident.

A few years earlier, in 1609, an Englishman named Henry Hudson had been hired by a Dutch trading company to search for a new trading route to Asia. Hudson had explored the coast of North America hoping to find a way to sail from the Atlantic Ocean to the Pacific Ocean so he could reach China and India. Dutch merchants traded with these countries and wanted Hudson to find a faster way to get goods from Asia to Europe.

Adriaen Block and his crew had to build shelters immediately in order to survive the long cold winter.

Henry Hudson traded with the Lenni-Lenape Indians who lived along the shores of New York Harbor.

Hudson never did find a route to Asia. He did discover that the local Lenni-Lenape Indians were friendly, skilled hunters, and more than willing to trade furs for manufactured goods such as pots and knives. Furs were very valuable in Europe. They were used to make clothes and hats.

Hudson claimed all the land nearby for the country of the Netherlands (also known as Holland) where his Dutch employers lived. He wrote in his journal, "It is as pleasant a land as one need tread upon. The land is the finest for cultivation that I ever in my life set foot upon." Then he returned home with stories of riches to be made in the New World. (Europeans called America the New World and Europe the Old World.)

Four years later, Adriaen Block heard about Hudson's discoveries and decided to try his luck trading in the New World. He sailed to New York Harbor and anchored near the island of Manhattan. At first, Block successfully traded with the Lenni-Lenape. Then his boat, the *Tiger,* caught fire.

Block and his crew tried to stop the raging flames, but they quickly were forced to abandon ship and swim for their lives. The explorers were now stranded thousands of miles from home. They had no ship and only a few supplies that they had rescued from the *Tiger*. To make matters worse, the fierce northeast winter was rapidly approaching.

Help From the Lenni-Lenape

Block was desperate. He and his men would starve or freeze to death if they did not find help. Block turned to the Lenni-Lenape. The Indians he had been trading with supplied his crew with food. They also helped Block and his men build simple log cabins to live in during the bitter, snowy winter.

Block's crew survived the winter and began building a new boat in the spring of 1614. They managed to put together a 40-foot (12-meter) sailing craft using materials and tools they had on hand. They called their new boat the *Onrust*, which means "restless" in Dutch.

Block knew that the tiny *Onrust* had no chance of sailing across the Atlantic Ocean to Holland. Instead, he decided to explore the local waters. Sailing up the river on the east side of Manhattan Island, Block and his crew soon reached Long Island **Sound**. Turning northeast, they crossed the sound and sailed along the southern coast of what would become Connecticut. Then Block steered his ship north up a very large river. He learned that the Indians in the area called the river Quinnehtukqut, which means "beside the long tidal river." When Europeans wrote the name down, they spelled it "Connecticut." This would become the name of the river and the territory that bordered it.

Exploring the River

Block sailed past deep woods on both riverbanks. After several days, he came to an Indian village. There, he met the Saukiog, who hunted, fished, and farmed along the Quinnehtukqut near present-day Hartford. Block and his crew stayed with the Saukiog for two weeks and then continued upriver. When the *Onrust* encountered powerful rapids swirling across the entire river, they were forced to return to Long Island Sound.

After exploring part of Rhode Island, Block and his weary crew met a European trading ship which finally carried them back home to Holland.

Block's tales of furs and friendly Indians brought additional Dutch traders to Connecticut. In 1633, the Dutch established a trading post near the Saukiog village that Block had visited. They called this trading post the House of Hope. The trading post was a small settlement set up to exchange manufactured goods from Europe for furs that the Indians trapped. A few Dutch traders stayed there for short periods of time and then returned home when they were finished trading. No Dutch people came to Connecticut to settle permanently.

Adriaen Block and his crew found passage home on a European sailing ship they came upon while exploring the coast of Connecticut.

At the time that Block was exploring the Connecticut River, the English had already set up two colonies nearby. These colonies were called Massachusetts Bay Colony and the Plymouth Plantation. Both colonies would eventually become part of the colony of Massachusetts.

Word soon spread to those colonies that the fur trade was good along the Connecticut River. The explorers who came to trade then discovered that the Connecticut River valley also had very fertile farmland. English people quickly began to view Connecticut as a good place to settle on farms. The arrival of English settlers in Connecticut had a huge effect on the lives of the Dutch traders and the Indian tribes in the region.

Quinnehtukqut

Long before any Europeans arrived in Connecticut, the area was home to many tribes of Native Americans. Although the tribes had individual names, they were all bound together by a common language, the Algonquian language. The Algonquian settled mainly on the coast and along the rivers of what is today the northeastern United States. In addition to a common language, the Algonquian tribes shared many customs and ways of life.

There were roughly sixteen Algonquian tribes living in Connecticut when the first Dutch explorers arrived. Most of Connecticut's Indian tribes clustered along the Quinnehtukqut and the northern coast of Long Island Sound. The Podunk and Saukiog lived along the Quinnehtukqut near the Dutch House of Hope trading post. The Pequot were the largest and most powerful tribe in the area. They lived near the Mystic River along the southeastern coast. The Mohegan lived north of the Pequot in the forests that bordered the Quinnehtukqut River. The villages of smaller tribes dotted the sound west of the Mystic River.

Many of the Native American tribes of Connecticut lived along rivers and streams where land was fertile and fish were abundant.

In all, there were 6,000 to 7,000 Native Americans in Connecticut in the mid-1600s. Historians believe that several decades earlier many more Indians had lived in the region. But in 1616 an epidemic swept through Connecticut and Massachusetts, killing thousands of Indians.

The epidemic was the result of disease, probably **smallpox** or **diphtheria**, brought to America by the first European explorers and settlers. Germs passed very quickly from the European traders to the defenseless Native Americans, who had no natural resistance to these diseases. Europeans had much greater resistance because they had been exposed to the diseases over generations. Outbreaks of smallpox and other diseases did sometimes kill large numbers of European settlers, but for the Indians these diseases were even more deadly. A simple handshake to seal a trade also sealed their fate. The epidemic of 1616 that wiped out thousands of Connecticut Indians was a deadly, if unintended, "gift" from their new European friends.

A Land of Great Beauty

Although most of Connecticut's Indians lived near the coast and rivers like the Quinnehtukqut, Connecticut was also filled with rolling hills covered in lush forests. Smaller rivers and streams cut through these forests. More than a thousand lakes dotted the hills. The Quinnehtukqut River valley provided the Indians with rich soil in which to grow crops. The nearby forests teemed with animals for them to hunt. The rivers, lakes, and sound were filled with fish.

Connecticut's Indian tribes were small and **mobile**. Each tribe had a territory with several village sites. They moved from one site to another as weather and food supplies changed.

In summer, the tribe would set up their houses, called wigwams, near the coast. There they planted corn, beans, and squash in fields surrounding their village. Women and children gathered clams, oysters, and lobsters from the shores of the sound. Men hunted ducks and other waterbirds that nested in the nearby marshes. They also used bows and arrows to hunt turkeys, squirrels, and other small animals in the forest. Paddling their canoes out into the sound, they caught fish using harpoons, fishing hooks, and nets.

When the weather turned cold, the people of the village would move away from the fierce storms and bitter winds that swept the coast. The houses were broken down, moved, and rebuilt in a sheltered valley. Plenty of firewood for the winter was available from the surrounding forests.

Tobacco

Most Algonquian people raised and smoked tobacco. The Indians considered the plant and the smoke sacred. It was smoked in pipes as part of religious ceremonies. The Algonquian thought the smoke carried their prayers and wishes to friendly spirits.

Native American men and women divided the work they needed to do to feed, clothe, and shelter their families.

As the temperature dropped and the snow began to fall, the men of the village turned their hunting skills toward larger animals. Deer, moose, and bears were easy to track in the snow, which slowed down the animals and made them easier to kill. The Indians hunted foxes, beavers, and otter in the winter when the coats of these animals were thickest. The women soaked the hides in a mixture of water and animal intestines to soften them. Then they fashioned the skins into warm clothes for the tribe.

Indian Homes

The Indians of Connecticut lived in lightweight, portable wigwams. These houses were made of poles covered with tree bark and sealed with mud and grass. They could be taken apart and put back together quickly as the tribe moved with the changing seasons. Parents, children, and grandparents often shared a single home. The houses were set up close together to form small villages.

Inside the house, animal skins covering the floor served as beds. Families gathered around the cooking fire to prepare meals and share stories. Women cooked, creating vegetable and meat stews made from the foods that the tribe grew, gathered, and hunted. Meals were eaten from bowls made of wood or clay. Utensils fashioned from wood and animal bones served as forks, knives, and spoons.

Each tribe was headed by a chief called a sachem. Although the sachem had the final word, other adults in the tribe, both men and women, also had a say in important matters. Most Connecticut tribes were friendly with each other. Different tribes traded and socialized together. An exception was the Pequot. This tribe had a reputation for being aggressive and for sometimes stealing other tribes' crops. Another tribe that was not always friendly was the Mohawk. This New York tribe sometimes raided Indian villages along the Connecticut River.

Different Views

Many of the Dutch and English people who came to Connecticut misunderstood the Indian way of life. The Algonquian did not place a high value on owning things. Native Americans valued sharing among the tribe rather than collecting personal wealth. This attitude was very different from the attitude of the Europeans who came to settle in Connecticut and the other colonies.

In Algonquian villages, men worked together to clear fields. They hunted and fished in groups. Whatever they caught was shared by the entire tribe. The women of the tribe worked side by side as a team to plant crops in the fields. They shared the tasks of tending the crops during the summer and harvesting them in the fall.

The newcomers from Europe did not understand these Indian beliefs and customs. They thought the Indians were poor because they did not collect individual possessions. In turn, the Native Americans did not understand why the settlers were so concerned about individual wealth.

Indian Pets

Many Indians kept dogs as pets. The dogs helped the Indians hunt and kept watch for wild animals while women worked in the fields. Families often had as many as six dogs.

In addition to dogs, some Indians kept pet hawks to scare crows and other birds away from their cornfields.

They wondered why these newcomers did not work together to grow crops and hunt. These differing viewpoints led to many misunderstandings and eventually caused wars between the settlers and the Indians.

Colonists Arrive

In the 1630s, English colonists settled in the Connecticut River valley and along the coast of Long Island Sound. They set up farms and built villages. The Indians living there greeted the newcomers as friends and trading partners. They hoped that the English would become their **allies** in their conflicts with more powerful Indian tribes.

At first, the colonists lived in peace with their new neighbors. But as time passed, disagreements over who owned the land led to fighting between the two groups.

In time, as the colony expanded, the Indians of Connecticut would be forced to give up their way of life. European colonists arrived in the New World armed with the belief that the land and everything in it was theirs for the taking. These newcomers drove the native people from their homes, destroyed their crops, and burned their villages. Many Indians died. Some Connecticut tribes were completely wiped out. The few remaining Indians were forced to adopt the new ways of the settlers who claimed the land as their own.

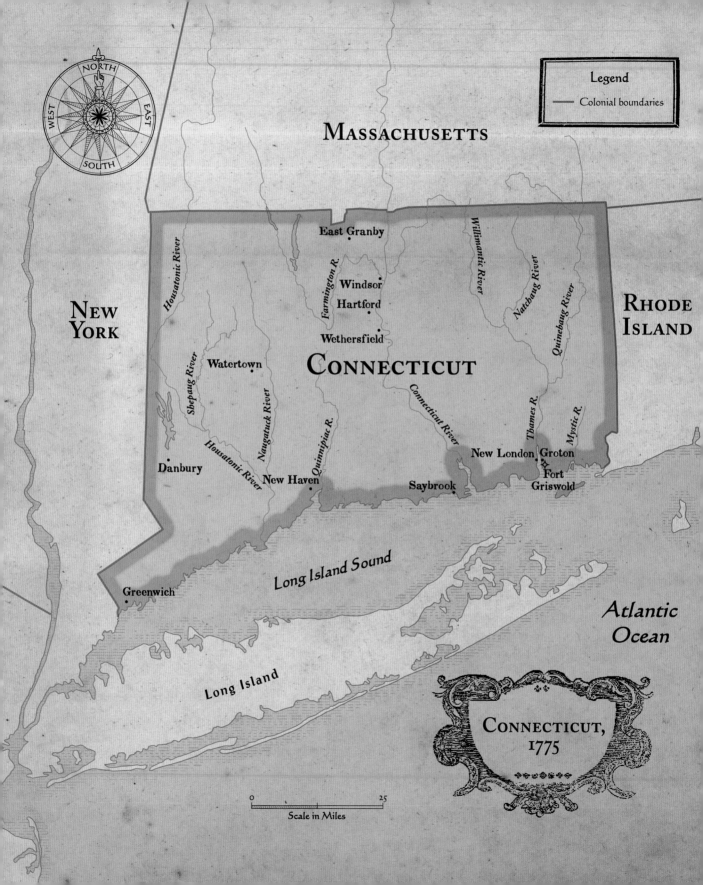

CHAPTER TWO

The First Settlers

The Puritans Arrive

Although the Dutch came upon Connecticut before other Europeans, they were much more interested in trading than in setting up permanent settlements. The English, on the other hand, wanted to colonize the New World. By 1631, they had already established several colonies in North America, including Massachusetts Bay Colony and Plymouth Plantation.

That year Chief Wahginnacut of the Podunk tribe visited these colonies. He told the English about the rich farmland along the Quinnehtukqut. Some colonists decided to move from their homes in Plymouth and Massachusetts to start new lives in Connecticut. These first English settlers belonged to a religious group called the Puritans. They were looking for more than just rich farmland in Connecticut. They were also hoping to find religious freedom.

This map shows how Connecticut looked in 1775.

Podunk

In 1631, Chief Wahginnacut of the Podunk tribe visited the English villages of Plymouth and Boston. The Podunk were a small tribe that lived along a river in Connecticut. Wahginnacut encouraged English settlers to come to the Quinnehtukqut valley. He told them of the fertile soil and the many animals to hunt that awaited them there. He also described the great village that the Podunk lived in.

Wahginnacut wanted the English to come to the area because he feared the Mohawk, a rival tribe that lived in eastern New York. The Mohawk regularly raided the villages of the Podunk and other small tribes in the area. Wahginnacut hoped that the English would fight the Mohawk and protect the Podunk.

When English settlers arrived, they found that the Podunk village was much smaller than they had imagined. From that point on, English settlers called any small, isolated town or village Podunk. The word has the same meaning today.

In the early 1600s, England had only one official religion. It was called the Church of England. Anyone who criticized the church or practiced another religion could be punished, even sent to jail. In spite of these dangers, many people in England spoke out against the church. They wished to worship in their own ways.

The Puritans were among the people who wanted to follow their own idea of worship. They believed the Church of England had become **corrupt**. They felt that it needed to be "purified." They started their own religion and called themselves Puritans. To escape punishment, the Puritans had to worship in secret.

After years of struggle, a group of Puritans decided to leave England in search of a place where they could freely practice their religion. This group of Puritans was called the Pilgrims. Boarding a ship called the *Mayflower*, they sailed for America in 1620. They intended to go to the already established English colony of Virginia. But strong winds in the North Atlantic Ocean blew them off course.

The Pilgrims in Plymouth

When the *Mayflower* finally landed, the Pilgrims found themselves in Cape Cod Bay north of Connecticut. This region had already been claimed by England and was run by a group of traders called the Plymouth Company.

The *Mayflower* arrived in mid-November. The weather was already extremely cold. Helped by local Indians, the Pilgrims built makeshift homes and gathered what food they could. Their first winter in America was a desperate struggle for survival. Almost half of them died before spring.

When warmer weather finally came, the survivors built a small town. Local Indians taught the Pilgrims how to plant corn and beans, how to fish the plentiful rivers, and how to hunt in the dense forests of the New World.

John Smith Names New England

John Smith was an English explorer and colonist. He founded Jamestown, Virginia, the first permanent English colony in America, in 1607. Smith was badly burned in an accident in 1609 and had to return to England. But he wanted to return to America when he recovered from his injury.

Smith's chance came in 1614, when he led an expedition to search for whales, animal furs, and new territory for the English to claim in America. His ship sailed along the coasts of Maine, New Hampshire, Massachusetts, Rhode Island, and Connecticut. During his journey, Smith created some of the first maps of the region and named the area New England. The name has been used to describe the northeastern portion of the United States ever since.

Puritan Problems

In time, the Pilgrims established a successful new colony. They survived hardship, began to build a new life, and were able to practice their religion as they chose. They called their new colony Plymouth Plantation.

In 1630, another group of Puritans followed. They landed north of Plymouth and settled in a new town called Boston and a new colony named Massachusetts Bay Colony. Other people seeking religious freedom soon came to these two colonies. Some of these new settlers were not

Puritans. They belonged to other religious groups like the Quakers. They brought their own view of Christianity to the New World.

As more and more people with other beliefs arrived, the Puritans feared that their own beliefs were being corrupted by these newcomers. In time, the Puritans became as **intolerant** toward other religions as the Church of England had been toward them. This was especially true in Boston. The Puritans threw out people who thought differently than they did. Many people, including some Puritans who disagreed with this intolerant attitude, left Massachusetts in search of religious freedom. This time they traveled to nearby areas in the New World, including Connecticut.

The First Connecticut Settlers

In 1633, a small group of Puritans from Plymouth decided to try their luck settling along the Connecticut River. They traveled overland carrying a house frame with them. When they reached a spot not far north of the House of Hope, they set up their house and quickly built a **stockade** to protect them from attacks by Indians or the Dutch traders to the south. They called their little settlement Windsor. During the next two years, Connecticut's first European colonists cleared fields and planted crops.

When the Puritans from Plymouth arrived in Connecticut, men, women, and children all helped to build the settlement.

Word of the success of the Windsor settlement spread through Plymouth and Massachusetts. In the summer of 1635, the original colonists were joined by a group of farmers from the town of Dorchester in the Massachusetts Bay Colony. More colonists arrived with their livestock in November of the same year. Nearly a hundred settlers now lived in the town. Things had gone well for them so far. That was about to change.

The winter of 1635 came early, and it was unusually cold. The settlers had planned for the winter and expected to receive supplies from a ship coming up the Connecticut River. Before the ship arrived, however, the river froze solid. Soon everyone in Windsor was in danger of starving.

The new settlers had to find their supply ship. Seventy men, women, and children decided to make the long, cold trek of nearly 50 miles (80 kilometers) down the banks of the Connecticut River to Long Island Sound. A few others remained in Windsor to try to survive the winter.

The settlers trudged through the bitter cold toward the river's mouth. Finally, they reached the sound. As they gazed over the frozen river, their supply ship was nowhere in sight. The settlers were starving and nearly frozen. But their luck had not quite run out.

Frozen in the ice was another ship called the *Rebecca*. The captain invited the Windsor colonists aboard and allowed them to stay until rains freed the ship from the ice. Then the settlers had to make a choice. They could stay and wait for their supply ship or return to Massachusetts on the *Rebecca*. After their ordeal, the settlers were too discouraged to risk staying behind. They abandoned their hopes of settling in Connecticut and sailed back to Boston.

As it turned out, most of those who remained in Windsor survived the tough winter after all. They had been helped by local Indians who provided them with food. However, many of their animals died from the cold. In spite of these hardships, in the spring of 1636, more colonists arrived from the town of Dorchester. The town of Windsor continued to grow even with all these troubles.

Two More Towns

There was so much fertile land along the Connecticut River that the area did not remain unsettled for long. Another group of Massachusetts colonists **migrated** to Connecticut in 1636. They were led by John Oldham, an explorer and trader from Massachusetts who had visited Connecticut in 1633. It was Oldham's reports of the Connecticut River valley that had encouraged the Dorchester colonists to move to Windsor. Oldham led his group south of Windsor and founded the town of Wethersfield. Within a year, 800 colonists had found their way into the Connecticut River valley and were living in and around the towns of Windsor and Wethersfield.

That same year, the Reverend Thomas Hooker led a group of about a hundred colonists from Massachusetts into Connecticut. Hooker was a Puritan pastor who believed that people should be able to worship as they pleased. He also believed that the government should be run by the people, not by a king. John Winthrop, the governor of Massachusetts, did not like Hooker's ideas. This pushed Hooker to look for a place where he and his followers could live as they chose.

Hooker's group found a place to build a new community very near the House of Hope between Windsor and

Wethersfield. They brought their cattle, goats, and pigs to help them establish farms. Legend says that Hooker's party lived on cow's milk and almost nothing else during the two-week journey. They named their new settlement Hartford.

Governor Winthrop wrote about the journey in his diary, dated May 31, 1636.

> *Mr. Hooker, pastor of the church of New Town and most of his congregation, went to Connecticut. His wife was carried in horses-litter; and they drove one hundred and sixty cattle, and fed of their milk by the way.*

Traveling from Massachusetts to Connecticut was a difficult two-week journey for the colonists who first settled Hartford.

The General Court

The towns of Windsor, Wethersfield, and Hartford were all located along the Connecticut River within 15 miles (24 kilometers) of each other. Together they were known as the Three River Towns. Soon the towns joined together to form the Connecticut Colony. They created a new government called the Connecticut General Court, made up of representatives from the three towns. It met for the first time in April 1636.

The new settlers kept watch in case of Indian attacks.

The General Court had very few duties and, for the most part, the towns operated on their own. The court made the sale of guns, gunpowder, and liquor to Indians illegal. It made new rules to prevent cows, pigs, and goats from running wild. The first settlers were much more concerned with planting crops, building houses, and surviving the coming winter than with government. But by banding together, Connecticut's towns had formed the beginnings of a new colony.

Saybrook Colony

The next settlement in Connecticut was started by its future governor. John Winthrop Jr. was the son of the governor of Massachusetts. The younger Winthrop was one of the richest and most important residents of Massachusetts. Along with other wealthy Massachusetts landowners, Winthrop wanted to establish a colony in Connecticut.

Winthrop knew that military control of the Connecticut River would be important to settlements in the area. In 1635, he sent a group of twenty men to take control of a point of land at the mouth of the river and build a settlement there. First, Winthrop's men threw out a group of Dutch traders who had set up a trading post on the point. The following year, they built a fort on the site. Winthrop named it Fort Saybrook after Lord Saye, one of the men who had given him money to set up a colony in Connecticut. Winthrop declared Saybrook a separate colony from Massachusetts and Connecticut.

Saybrook was the fourth permanent town in what would become Connecticut Colony. But Saybrook was more of a trading post than a real village. The fort had only one permanent resident, a man named George Fenwicke. Winthrop had sent Fenwicke to run the fort and trading post. Saybrook did not join the other towns as part of Connecticut Colony until 1644.

The Pequot War

In 1636, a man named John Oldham was sailing near Block Island (named for Adriaen Block). He was attacked and killed by Indians. The discovery of his mangled body caused an outcry in Boston and the river towns. An investigation revealed that the Indians of the Manissean tribe from Block Island had killed Oldham. However, when a group of Connecticut **militia** from Hartford tried to capture the Manissean Indians, the Pequot Indians hid them and refused to turn them over. As far as the colonists were concerned, the Pequot were now as guilty as the Manissean Indians.

For the next two years, the Pequot and settlers fought each other. The Indians attacked the fort at Saybrook repeatedly and the settlers shot Pequot whenever they encountered them. Lion Gardner, who was in charge of the fort, was not happy about the militia attacking the Pequot and then returning to Hartford. "You have come to raise a nest of hornets about our ears, and then you will flee away," he wrote to the militia in Hartford. But the attacks continued back and forth.

Then, in April 1637, a band of Pequot paddled up the Connecticut River to Wethersfield. They attacked farmers working in the fields and killed at least six men and three women. They captured two other young women. When the Indians passed Fort Saybrook, they raised poles from their canoes with the captives' clothes on them.

The attack on Wethersfield and the kidnapping of the two women outraged the settlers in Connecticut. In May 1637, the General Court at Hartford took swift action. It sent a militia force of ninety men from the towns of Wethersfield, Windsor, and Hartford to destroy Pequot villages. They were joined by reinforcements from Massachusetts and a group of Mohegan and Narragansett Indians who were friendly with the settlers. The force, which now numbered almost 400, was led by a militia captain named John Mason.

Mason's army boarded boats and sailed to Narragansett Harbor, where one of two Pequot **strongholds** was located. The Indian village was surrounded by a **palisade** designed to protect those inside from harm. In the battle to come, the high fence would have the opposite effect.

The militia surrounded the village and began firing muskets at the Indians inside. Mason grabbed a torch from a nearby cooking fire and tossed it onto a wigwam. The house burst into flames, and the fire quickly spread to other houses. Soon every house in the village was burning. Any Pequot who tried to escape through the narrow palisade gate was shot. Between 600 and 700 Indian men, women, and children were killed by bullets or by fire.

Captain Mason summed up the battle:

And thus in little more than one Hour's space was their impregnable Fort with themselves utterly Destroyed, to the number of six or seven Hundred, as some of themselves confessed. There were only seven taken Captive & about seven escaped.

The Pequot who lived in other villages fled for their lives. The militia quickly got reinforcements and chased them across Connecticut. The Indians, carrying their children, moved slowly. As a result, the militia quickly caught up with them. Most of the Indians were either killed or captured. One of the few to escape was the Pequot chief, Sassacus. He fled north into New York but was soon captured by Mohawks. His head was sent to Mason as a gift of peace from the Mohawk tribe.

In 1637, John Mason and a militia numbering 400 men attacked and destroyed the Pequot Indian village on Narragansett Harbor.

The few remaining Pequot were made servants of the settlers or sold as slaves to other Indian tribes. From that time forward, the Indians of Connecticut did not challenge the European newcomers as they expanded their farms and villages. The settlers had proved that they could be a powerful ally and an even more powerful and destructive enemy.

The Pequot War ended the traditional way of life for many of Connecticut's native people. The war would also change how Connecticut's settlers governed themselves.

CHAPTER THREE

The Colony Takes Shape

A New Outlook

After the Pequot War, every able-bodied man in Connecticut over the age of sixteen was ordered to train in the militia for ten days per year. This strengthened the military. In addition, Connecticut's leaders thought that the colony needed a different form of government. At the time, most settlers in the colony were Puritans. Puritans believed that their leaders had been chosen by God. This meant that the leaders should be followed without question. This belief gave Puritan leaders almost complete control over the lives of their followers.

After the war with the Pequot, every man over the age of sixteen who lived in Connecticut had to train for the militia.

One Puritan who disagreed with this idea was the Reverend Thomas Hooker, founder of the town of Hartford. Hooker believed that government should be based on "the free consent of the people." People should choose their leaders. If allowed to do so, they would be loyal to them and follow their directions. In May 1638, Hooker outlined his ideas in a sermon. Some people were shocked when they heard or later read his words. Others were inspired to think about government in new ways. Hooker's sermon had a powerful effect on the people of Connecticut. It would shape the colony's new government.

The Fundamental Orders

During the next year, the General Court met to debate and discuss a new set of laws for Connecticut. In 1639, the court adopted the new laws, called the Fundamental Orders.

The Fundamental Orders outlined the basic laws that would govern Connecticut Colony. The Fundamental Orders stated that the people had the right to vote directly for their leaders and that colonists should be loyal to their colony, not to the king of England. This idea was very different from the way most people of the time thought about government and the loyalty they owed to it. The Fundamental Orders established Connecticut's legislature, or lawmaking body, and stated that a governor should be chosen by the people to oversee the colony. The governor was only allowed to serve two terms so as not to become too powerful.

Even though the Fundamental Orders were a great step toward **democratic** rule, they did not give everyone the right to vote. Only "Godly adult males who owned property" could vote or hold public office. This meant that only a few select men qualified as voters. Most men and all women, Native Americans, and blacks had no say in their government. Even with these limits, the Fundamental Orders gave Connecticut's citizens more freedom and more control of their government than most other people in the world had at that time.

The First Constitution

Connecticut is sometimes called the Constitution State. The nickname comes from the Fundamental Orders. This document is considered by many to be the first written **constitution** in America. The Fundamental Orders outlined the basic principles that would later become part of the U.S. Constitution.

- Government authority comes from the people.
- There shall be no taxation without representation.
- The number of government representatives should be determined by the population.
- All free people shall have the right to vote.

New Haven Colony

While Connecticut Colony was working on the Fundamental Orders, new settlers were moving into the nearby territory. After the Pequot War, word quickly spread that Connecticut was free of any threat from Indians. Soon more colonists streamed into the area, mostly from Massachusetts. Most of these new settlers were looking for new opportunities or religious freedom.

Two new arrivals to Boston in 1637 also set their sights on Connecticut. One was a Puritan minister named John Davenport. The other, Theophilus Eaton, was a wealthy merchant from London, England. Davenport had come to Boston from England with a group of followers. They wanted to live in a place where their strict Puritan ideas would not be challenged. Eaton was a member of Davenport's church and had been persuaded by the pastor to help finance the journey to America.

After only a few months in Boston, both men decided to search for a new place to settle. They heard reports from soldiers returning from the Pequot War about a place called Quinnipiac in southern Connecticut. Eaton decided to take a few followers and investigate. Eaton's group found what they thought would be the ideal location for a new town where the Quinnipiac River flowed into Long Island Sound.

Eaton returned to Boston and told Davenport that he had found the perfect place for their new settlement. In April 1638, Davenport's flock sailed from Boston and arrived at the Quinnipiac River. They set up temporary shelters by digging cellars and covering them with wooden and thatched roofs. The cellars must have been dark and damp compared to the comfortable homes in London that the settlers had left only a few months before. But the new colonists worked hard and built large houses within a few years. Davenport's house was built in the shape of a cross. Eaton's was built in the shape of an *E*. It had nineteen fireplaces.

Minister John Davenport and his followers settled along the Quinnipiac River in spring of 1638.

At first, the new colony was called Quinnipiac, but in 1640 the name was changed to New Haven. The colonists bought sizable tracts of land from the local Indians. Unlike many settlers in Connecticut and the other colonies, the New Haven colonists allowed the Indians to continue to hunt and fish on the land. Overall, New Haven's settlers treated the Indians fairly and had good relationships with them.

Davenport declared that his new settlement was a separate colony from Massachusetts and Connecticut. Davenport adopted a set of laws for the colony that strictly followed Puritan religious teachings. The colony was governed by seven church leaders called the Seven Pillars. Davenport and Eaton called their colony the "Bible State" because it was based on their strict Puritan beliefs. New settlers who wanted to live in religious surroundings soon came to join Davenport in New Haven.

The Colonies Expand

Connecticut now had three separate English colonies: Connecticut Colony (which included the three river towns of Windsor, Wethersfield, and Hartford), Saybrook, and New Haven. Saybrook joined with the river towns and became part of Connecticut Colony in 1644. In time, all three colonies would unite to form one. But in the mid-1600s, there was still much room for growth.

By 1670, colonists had well-established towns all along Long Island Sound and the Connecticut River, where the families of farmers and tradesmen thrived.

With the Indian threat gone, more settlers moved to Connecticut. The population grew rapidly from about 1,000 settlers at the end of the Pequot War to more than 20,000 by 1670. At first, new colonists settled near the existing towns. But soon they began to spread out. New towns sprang up along Long Island Sound and the shores of the Connecticut River in both the Connecticut and New Haven colonies. Soon these colonies consisted of seven to ten towns each.

Each town had its own local government. One of the town government's most important jobs was to divide land among the residents. The towns worked out a system called "sizing." A committee of town sizers decided how much land each family would get. If the land was far from town, the family would get more land to make up for the distance they had to travel. Land near town was more valuable, so families would get smaller parcels.

A plot of land in the center of town was set aside for everyone's use. It was called the common. The town church or meetinghouse was built there along with a general store and often a tavern or inn. The town common was often at a crossroads.

Colonists gathered on the common to hear news about new laws and social issues of the day.

As Connecticut's towns grew, the settlers built larger houses and improved their school system. School was important to the Puritans because they believed that all children should be able to read and understand the Bible. In 1650, Connecticut Colony passed a law that required towns with more than fifty families to have an elementary school. Towns of one hundred or more families had to provide a secondary (high) school for older children.

Puritan Families

In the 1600s, most settlers in Connecticut were Puritans. Some followed the very strict religious beliefs of the New Haven colony. Others were less religious, but they still followed basic Puritan beliefs. These included Puritan ideas about family life.

The center of Puritan life was the family. The father was the head of the household. He was expected to be strict and to make all the important decisions. In addition, he was legally responsible for the behavior of all his children. If a child misbehaved or got into trouble, the father could be punished.

Women were expected to obey their husbands and could not own property on their own. Puritans believed that women should concern themselves only with raising children and maintaining the family home.

Children were expected to obey their parents without question. By the age of seven, every child was expected to do some useful work around the house. Girls were only allowed to learn housework, child care, and other skills for keeping a home. They could not have jobs in the community. Most Puritan girls were married by age sixteen and began having children soon afterwards. Puritan families often had six or eight children. Medical care was very limited and many young women died in childbirth.

Tombstones

When Connecticut colonists were buried, their graves were marked with gravestones, also called tombstones. Most tombstones were rectangular and many were elaborately carved. The most popular symbol carved into colonial gravestones was a skull with wings. It symbolized the flight of the soul from the body. In addition, many tombstones had poems about the person in the grave. Here is one example:

Under this sod and under those trees,
Here lies the body of Solomon Pease.
The peas are not here,
There's only the pod.
The peas shelled out and went up to God.

Boys were required to learn a trade or become farmers. Some boys went to work for a skilled tradesman as an apprentice by the age of twelve. They worked for a master craftsman, such as a carpenter, blacksmith, barrel maker, or wheel maker, for seven years to learn his trade. The apprentice often lived in his master's shop, sleeping on the floor or on a small cot. When his apprenticeship was over, the young man could open his own shop, begin working for himself, and perhaps start his own family.

Most Puritan families lived a strict, simple life. Both adults and children were expected to follow the rules and conform to the ways of the community. People worked many hours, six days a week, to provide for their families. Everyone attended church on the Sabbath, which began at sundown on Saturday and ended at sundown on Sunday. Church services lasted most of the day and the sermon was often two to three hours long. Men sat on one side of the church and women on the other. Children and servants sat in the back. Those who fell asleep or misbehaved were rapped on the head with a long pole.

The Puritan families of Connecticut did have a few opportunities for fun and games. At town meetings, weddings, and on election day, families gathered to enjoy themselves. However, daily life was slow and steady for most of Connecticut's Puritan settlers. As a result, the colony became known as the Land of Steady Habits.

The New England Confederation

The Pequot War scared the leaders of Connecticut. They were afraid that another conflict with the Indians might occur. Also, they feared that the large Dutch colony of New Netherland, in what is now New York, might try to take some or all of their territory. The Dutch had set up the first settlement in Connecticut at the House of Hope and still had traders and some troops there. The General Court of Connecticut decided it had to protect the colony from the Dutch.

In 1643, Connecticut Colony, New Haven, Massachusetts Bay Colony, and Plymouth Plantation formed an **alliance** called the New England Confederation. The purpose of the alliance was to protect the four colonies from attack by Indians or the Dutch. They agreed to help each other in case one was attacked, just as Massachusetts and Connecticut had helped each other during the Pequot War. The colonies kept their own governments but formed a council with two **representatives** each. They agreed that no colony could go to war unless at least six of the eight representatives voted for it.

The New England Confederation lasted for forty years. It proved that the colonies could cooperate with each other and form a joint government. It was the first time that colonies in America joined together to protect each other. All thirteen colonies would join together in a similar union more than one hundred years later to fight for their freedom from England.

The Connecticut Charter

The Fundamental Orders gave Connecticut Colony a stable form of government. And the New England Confederation gave security to the colony in case of attack by Indians or another colony such as New Netherland. There was only one thing missing. The leaders of the Connecticut Colony worried that they did not have a legal right to the colony after all.

Leaders from towns in the Connecticut Colony gathered to discuss the need for a charter from the king of England.

England had claimed the territory of Connecticut, but so had Holland. Connecticut's leaders wanted to be sure that England would protect them in case Holland or another country tried to take Connecticut by force. They needed an official document from the English king stating that Connecticut was an English colony. Such a document was called a charter.

In 1662, the leaders of the colony decided to send John Winthrop Jr. to England to ask Charles II, the king of England, for a charter. Winthrop had been elected governor of Connecticut in 1657. He was so popular that the colony's leaders **repealed** a law in the Fundamental Orders that limited governors to only two terms in office. As a result, Winthrop remained in office for almost twenty years.

Winthrop made the long journey by ship to London, the capital of England. He took along a copy of the Fundamental Orders. Winthrop hoped that the king would base the charter on the Fundamental Orders so that Connecticut's government would remain unchanged. It would just have the protection of the English army in case of attack.

The Charter Is Signed

In London, Winthrop met with the king and his advisers for several months to discuss the charter. In April 1662, the king signed Connecticut's charter. It granted Connecticut's settlers many rights to self-government. The colony would be run by a governor, deputy governor, and twelve assistants. There also would be an elected assembly to make laws and a court system to enforce them. Winthrop was appointed Connecticut's first governor under the new charter.

In addition, the charter set Connecticut's boundaries. The colony would include not only the area occupied by the three river towns, but also New Haven Colony and parts of Rhode Island, Massachusetts, Pennsylvania, and New Netherland. In fact, the king extended Connecticut's western border all the way to the Pacific Ocean. That made the colony about 60 miles (96 kilometers) from north to south and almost 3,000 miles (4,800 kilometers) from east to west.

At first, the people of New Haven Colony were very unhappy that their colony was included in the charter. But in 1665, they finally agreed to become part of Connecticut. With the new charter in place, Connecticut was now a united colony. Connecticut would need the strength of all its people to face the tests that lay ahead.

Colonists gathered to hear news of the new charter.

CHAPTER FOUR

Times of Conflict

King Philip's War

Soon after Connecticut received its charter in 1662, the new colony was faced with two big challenges. An Indian war threatened its peace and a new English king tried to take away its charter. The citizens of Connecticut would unite to overcome both challenges.

The Indian tribes of New England had many reasons to hate the white settlers. The colonists had driven them from their lands and brought disease that killed thousands of Native Americans. Following the end of the Pequot War in 1637, most Indian people in the New England colonies feared the colonists. The Indian population was growing smaller while more and more colonists were moving into the territory. Most Indians feared that if they fought the colonists they would face the same fate as the Pequot.

During the late 1600s, Indian tribes wanted revenge for mistreatment by the settlers and attacked the colonists.

King Philip's War ended any threat of Indian uprising in New England. To the Puritans, Metacomet symbolized the devil. To his Indian allies, he was a great hero who tried to recover lands that had been stolen from them. In the end, the Indians lost their lands and were forced to change their way of life.

A Threat From England

Connecticut had helped overcome the challenge of King Philip's War. Soon it faced another challenge to its existence. The new threat came from another English colony and from England itself.

In 1665, King Charles II took over the Dutch colony of New Netherland. He gave the colony to his brother James, the Duke of York, and renamed it New York. Now there was another English colony directly west of Connecticut. At first, this seemed like a good thing because Connecticut's leaders had always feared and mistrusted the Dutch. There had been many disputes over land between Connecticut and the Dutch of New Netherland. Now Connecticut had an ally instead of an enemy on its western border.

Things went well for nearly ten years. Then, in 1674, King Charles granted New York a new charter. The charter gave New York all the land west of the Connecticut River. This included nearly half of Connecticut Colony.

Connecticut's leaders protested to Sir Edmund Andros, the governor of New York. But Andros would not listen and decided to take the territory by force.

Andros loaded soldiers onto ships and sailed to Saybrook at the mouth of the Connecticut River. His men surrounded the fort and demanded that the Connecticut militia surrender. Captain Thomas Bull was commander of the Connecticut troops guarding the fort. Bull refused to give up Saybrook.

The Connecticut militia and its leaders stood their ground when Sir Edmund Andros attempted to take the territory by force.

Andros offered Bull a bribe, but that did not work either. It was clear to Andros that he would have to fight to take over Saybrook and western Connecticut. Andros had second thoughts and finally gave up. Without firing a single shot,

Andros and his men returned to New York. Connecticut had stood its ground and kept the colony together.

Andros later contacted John Winthrop, the governor of Connecticut. The two men were able to settle the dispute peacefully. Connecticut gave up its claims to some towns along the New York border, and New York agreed to give up its claim to the territory west of the Connecticut River. The crisis was over for now. But Andros would return ten years later to claim the whole colony.

The Dominion of New England

In 1685, King Charles II of England died. His brother James, the Duke of York, became King James II. Now James owned not only the colony of New York, but all of the English colonies in America. He had new ideas about how to run these colonies. In 1686, King James decided to combine the colonies of Connecticut, Massachusetts, New Hampshire, Rhode Island, and Plymouth into one "supercolony" called the Dominion of New England. Its capital would be Boston, and Sir Edmund Andros would be the governor.

One of Andros's first acts was to demand that all of the New England colonies turn over their charters to him. His view was that the colonies no longer existed as separate governments. Therefore, they had no right to their charters.

He decided to go to Hartford himself to take Connecticut's charter from the assembly and Governor Winthrop. On October 31, 1687, with a bodyguard of seventy-five soldiers, Andros marched into Hartford. The events that followed would make this a Halloween to remember.

The Charter Oak Story

The story of what happened to Connecticut's charter when Andros and his men arrived in Hartford became a legend in the colony. Some parts of the story may be overstated, but it shows how strongly Connecticut colonists felt about their rights.

According to legend, Andros marched into the Chamber of the Assembly, the place where the charter was kept. The charter was brought out and laid on a table. Members of Connecticut's assembly made speeches against taking the charter. As the day wore on, it became dark inside the council chamber. Candles were lit and the speeches continued.

Then a member of the assembly named Andrew Leete rose to speak. Leete was in poor health, and as he leaned on the table, he slipped and knocked over the candles.

(Many people think he slipped intentionally.) Other candles in the chamber also went out. When the candles were finally relit, the charter was gone. Members of the assembly had handed the charter out a window to Captain Joseph Wadsworth, who slid it under his coat. He then hid the charter in a hollow in an oak tree.

Andros was furious. He declared that the government of Connecticut under the charter was ended. But there was nothing else he could do. Andros and his men returned to New York angry and without the charter. The records of the General Court for October 31, 1687, describe what happened but do not give the details.

At a General Court in Hartford, October 31st, 1687, his excellency, Sir Edmund Andros...took into his hands the government of the colony of Connecticut, it being by His Majesty annexed to Massachusetts and other colonies under His excellency's government.

According to these official records, the General Court did as the king wished. It turned over the government of Connecticut to Andros and the colony became part of the Dominion of New England. But the General Court had won a victory by keeping the colony's charter.

The tree in which Wadsworth hid the charter became known as the Charter Oak. It stood in Hartford until it was blown down in a storm in 1856. The charter can be found today displayed in Connecticut's capitol building.

Soon after the Charter Oak incident, Andros moved the capital of the Dominion of New England to Boston. For the next year, he ruled the Dominion from there. But his reign would not last long. King James's plan to combine the New England colonies came to a sudden end in 1688, when James was overthrown and a new king and queen came to rule in England. They did not agree with James's decision to take away the charters of the American colonies to create one large colony.

When this news reached Boston, Andros was arrested and sent back to England. But the governor never made it home. His ship was lost in a storm and everyone aboard, including Andros, drowned. Soon, the New England colonies, including Connecticut, returned to governments under their individual charters.

The Great Oak

The oak tree in which Connecticut's charter was hidden had a long history in the colony. The oak stood on a hill overlooking the Connecticut River. It was estimated to be about 500 years old when Joseph Wadsworth hid the charter inside.

Captain Adriaen Block had spotted the oak from his ship as he sailed up the river in 1614. The Saukiog invited him to sit beneath the oak when he traded with them. The tree was sacred to the Indians. It helped them know when to plant their crops. They knew it was time to plant when the oak leaves were the size of a mouse's ear.

The French and Indian War

Beginning in 1689, the countries of England and France began a series of four wars that would change American history. The wars started the year after Andros was sent back to England and Connecticut regained its charter. The two countries fought over the land each controlled in America. England now had thirteen colonies, including Connecticut, along the Atlantic coast of North America. France controlled what is now Canada and much of the territory to the west of the English colonies. The French called their American colony New France. Both countries wanted to control the whole continent.

Between 1689 and 1754, the French and English fought three wars in America. They were known as King William's War, Queen Anne's War, and King George's War. In each of these conflicts, the French had the help of Indian tribes, especially the Iroquois. The English sent troops to America to fight the French and got soldiers from the thirteen colonies to join the army. Connecticut contributed hundreds of soldiers to help the English fight the French. Some battles came as close to Connecticut as Massachusetts, but none were actually fought in the colony.

After the three conflicts lasting more than fifty years, both sides had gained almost nothing. The boundaries of their territories in America were about the same as when the wars began. But the fourth and final war between the French and English would change all that.

The final war in America between England and France began in 1754. Both France and England wanted to control the territory in western Pennsylvania along the Ohio River. The French began building forts in this area, and the English sent troops to stop them. The conflict began when a young lieutenant named George Washington was sent to the Ohio River valley to capture a French fort. Washington and his troops were defeated. This small but important battle touched off a conflict that would last nine years.

The Beginning of the End

England became determined not only to control the Ohio River, but to drive the French from America. To accomplish this goal, it sent thousands of soldiers from England. Many more joined from the thirteen colonies. During the conflict, Connecticut sent several thousand troops to fight against the French and their Indian allies. Once again, no fighting occurred on Connecticut land. But Connecticut militia fought in nearby New York and Massachusetts.

The French and Indian War dragged on for nine years. At first, the French defeated the English in almost every struggle. Thousands of English and colonial troops died in battle and from harsh winter conditions. Finally, in 1760, after the French had been pushed back to their territory in what is now Canada, English troops captured the capital of New France at Montreal.

A young lieutenant colonel from Connecticut named Israel Putnam played an important part in the takeover of Montreal. Putnam led a group of soldiers who captured two French ships by swimming out and boarding them. Putnam's military skills would be put to use again in the American Revolution.

The capture of Montreal ended the fighting in the French and Indian War. Three years later, France and England signed a treaty that turned over all of New France to England. The English now controlled all of North America. They had won the war, but the cost had been very high. The English had borrowed money from other countries to pay for the troops and supplies needed to defeat the French. The English government needed some way to pay this money back. They decided to collect the money from the thirteen colonies in America. This decision would lead to an even larger conflict than the French and Indian War.

Musical Signals

There were no radios, walkie-talkies, or cell phones in the colonial army. Signals were passed by shouting orders or by using musical instruments. Combinations of drums, flutes, and other instruments passed the message along in a kind of musical code.

Young men in their teens or even younger served as musicians in the army. This was a dangerous job. They had to march onto the battlefield with the other soldiers and play their instruments to tell the troops how and where to move.

Soldiers marching into battle during the French and Indian War were directed where to move by musicians who marched along with them.

Everyday Objects

Hunting

The Connecticut River valley was rich with wildlife. Lakes and streams overflowed with fish. Native American hunters used the spoils of this land to trade with European explorers.

꙰ Europeans used muskets for hunting.

꙰ Gunpowder for rifles was often carried in a hollowed-out horn fitted with a shoulder sling.

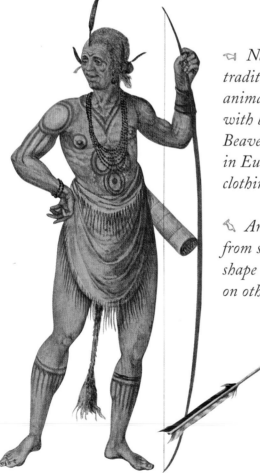

꙰ Native Americans traditionally hunted animals such as beavers with bows and arrows. Beaver fur was used in Europe to make clothing and hats.

꙰ Arrows were made from stones chiseled into shape and sharpened on other rocks.

꙰ Native Americans armed with muskets and bows and arrows would surround a beaver dam, waiting for the animals to emerge.

64

& *Trapping*

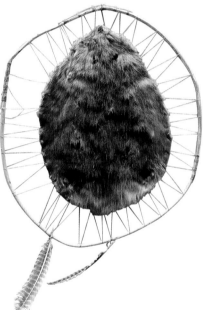

Beaver skins were stretched and dried on frames made from saplings. Once dry, the back side was rubbed on rough bark to remove any unwanted remains of the animal.

Europeans learned from Native Americans how to travel quietly along rivers in canoes.

Indians traded pelts for muskets, gunpowder, pots and pans, and blankets.

Europeans used steel traps to catch river otters. Otter fur was used by Europeans for clothing.

65

CHAPTER FIVE

A Thriving Colony

The Colony Grows

In 1756, Connecticut Colony took a **census** of its population. The census revealed that about 127,000 white people, about 3,000 black people, and 617 Indians lived in the colony. The colony was the fifth largest of the thirteen colonies.

About 90 percent of Connecticut's people lived and worked on small farms. These farmers had great success growing crops such as corn, wheat, peas, and tobacco. In addition, fishermen sailed from Connecticut's towns along the coast. They caught tons of fish from Long Island Sound. Large ships from the colony sailed the Atlantic Ocean in search of whales, which were in great demand. Whale oil was used in lamps. Umbrellas and clothing were made from whalebone.

A typical Connecticut town expanded as it became more prosperous.

Connecticut's farmers, fishermen, and tradesmen were growing, catching, and making more goods than they could possibly use. So they sent the extras to New York and Boston for sale. In return, they received manufactured goods such as clothing and tools.

Connecticut's small towns had grown in population during the hundred years since the first settlers founded them. There were now about seventy towns scattered throughout the colony. Yet in many ways Connecticut's towns had changed little. There were more buildings than in the 1600s, but the center of the Connecticut town was still the common. The town church, or sometimes more than one church, was located on the common. Some towns had a general store where colonists could buy almost anything they needed. In addition, there was often a blacksmith's shop, a school, and an inn or tavern.

Farms and Small Towns

Family farms surrounded the typical Connecticut town. Many Connecticut families were large, with eight or nine children. Parents, children, grandparents, aunts, uncles, and cousins often lived together in the same farmhouse. The houses were similar to those built by the first Puritan settlers. They were made from wood and had **clapboard** or shingle siding. Some of the original settlers' houses were still being used by their descendants a hundred years after they were built. As families grew, additional rooms were added to the houses, but most houses were still very crowded. It was rare for family members, especially children, to have their own bedrooms.

There was no indoor plumbing in colonial America. Water from an outside well was used for washing and cooking. Children were often given the job of carrying buckets of water into the house from the well. In winter, colonists had to break the ice that formed on the surface of the well water.

Survival on the farm meant that everyone in the family had to do a fair share of the work. Men and boys cleared the land, chopped firewood, plowed the fields, dug ditches, built houses and barns, and made furniture. They also hunted and fished. In the fall, men harvested the crops and carried any extra crops to town for sale. They traded these for things they could not make themselves, like sugar, spices, glassware, tools, guns, and ammunition.

Young boys helped their fathers with tilling and planting the fields for harvest.

Women and girls did the cooking, gardening, spinning, and housework. They also made most of the family's clothes from cloth they wove themselves. After the harvest in the fall, women cooked and sealed vegetables and fruits in glass or pottery jars to preserve them. Meat was dried and salted to make it last. Because there was no refrigeration and the shops in town did not sell groceries, preserving food was a vital chore to make sure the family had enough to eat through the long winter.

Because there were few doctors in Connecticut at this time, the woman of the house provided medical care. She often made her own medicines from herbs and other plants grown in the family garden or found in the forest.

Home Remedies

There were few doctors in Connecticut in colonial times. Illness and injury were treated with home remedies. These are a few remedies colonial mothers used to cure common ailments:

Asthma: Put a muskrat pelt on your chest, furry side down.

Chicken pox: Lie down in the chicken house until a black hen walks over you.

Headache: Put a buckwheat cake on your head until the pain goes away.

Toothache: Prick your tooth with a pine tree sliver, or spread fresh cow manure on your face.

Warts: Rub a potato on the warts and then bury the potato, or spit on the warts every morning.

Small children gathered firewood, shelled peas, and shucked corn. They also fed the chickens, milked the cows, and chased birds away from the family's crops.

Farm families worked from sunrise to sunset. At night, they gathered around the fireplace to talk, tell stories, or play games. The evening often ended with the father reading aloud from the Bible. Most families went to sleep early because they had to get up the next day to start work all over again.

An old New England saying sums up the way hard-working Connecticut farm families lived:

Use it up, wear it out,

Make it do, or do without.

Going to School

Every Connecticut town with more than fifty families was required to have an elementary school. Colonial children got up before dawn to do farm chores before walking to town to attend school. Classes were held in one-room schoolhouses where children of all ages would learn together. Older children often helped out by teaching younger students.

School rules were strict. Teachers could punish students who misbehaved by hitting them on the knuckles with a wooden stick. Most children attended school through the eighth grade. By the time they were teenagers, boys and girls were expected to spend their time working on family farms, in their fathers' businesses, or helping their mothers with household chores.

Only wealthy male students moved on to secondary (high) school. Even fewer students went to college. Latin, Greek, and other advanced subjects were taught to boys in the secondary schools. Most girls were only taught the basics of reading, writing, and arithmetic. If parents wanted a daughter to receive a more advanced education, they hired a private tutor.

Young children out of school found time for play while doing their chores around the barn.

Books and Newspapers

Because nearly every child in Connecticut learned to read, most families owned at least one book. The most popular book of the time was the Bible. As time passed, more books became available. Families began to have libraries that included English novels like *Gulliver's Travels* and *Robinson Crusoe.*

Many farm families also had an almanac. These books contained valuable information for farmers, such as sunrise and sunset times for the coming year, weather predictions, and suggestions about when to plant crops.

Connecticut did not have its own newspaper until 1755, when James Parker founded the *Connecticut Gazette* in Hartford. In 1764, the *Connecticut Courant* was started. This newspaper is still published today as the *Hartford Courant* and is the oldest continuously published newspaper in America.

Before Connecticut had its own newspapers, people picked up news from travelers or by reading newspapers from New York or Massachusetts. The news was often weeks or months old by the time it reached Connecticut's distant farms and villages. People who did not know how to read sat in taverns and inns and listened as others read aloud. Newspapers and pamphlets played an important role in binding Connecticut's citizens together and spreading new ideas about freedom throughout the colony. In fact, a tax on printed documents such as newspapers would start Connecticut and the other colonies on the road to revolution.

A Man of Words

One of Connecticut's most famous citizens was born in 1758. His name was Noah Webster. In 1783, Webster published a book called *Webster's Elementary Spelling Book* or *The Blue-Backed Speller*. His book sold more copies at the time than any book except the Bible. Webster published *An American Dictionary of the English Language* in 1828. This was the first major dictionary of American English. His name lives on in Webster's dictionaries today.

The Rise of Manufacturing

Around 1750, an important change occurred in Connecticut: small factories began to appear along Connecticut's many streams and rivers. Colonists began manufacturing goods in addition to farming and fishing. Until that time, most manufactured goods came to the colonies from England.

Small towns grew as new factories located there. Connecticut's factories turned out many different types of goods, such as hats, clocks, tinware, and cannons. Watertown became known as Brass City because of the many brass factories located there. Windsor was well known for making clocks. The first hat factory in America was started in Wethersfield. Soon, Connecticut was selling manufactured goods to the other colonies and even to England.

As trade within communities grew, business thrived. Some colonists became store owners, merchants, or manufacturers. Some entered the shipping business. By the mid-1700s, Connecticut colonists owned about seventy ships. Shipbuilding became an important industry along the coast of Long Island Sound. As towns grew, so did the need for more professional people, such as lawyers, bookkeepers, and doctors.

Yankees

Today when people refer to Yankees, they are most often talking about the New York baseball team. But the term *Yankee* began as a nickname for people from Connecticut and the rest of New England. There are several theories about how the word came to be. It may have come from the Scottish word *yankee*, meaning a clever woman. It might be a variation of Jan Kees (pronounced yahn-keez), the name the Dutch gave to the English in Connecticut.

Yankee Peddlers

Manufactured goods were sold in shops in towns throughout the colony. But most people still lived on farms and had to travel long distances to get to a town. To reach these customers, merchants loaded their goods onto horse-drawn carts and traveled out to the farms.

These salesmen were called "Yankee peddlers." They sold an amazing variety of goods, including pots, buttons, cloth, combs, medicine, tools, and almost every imaginable household item. The arrival of a new peddler in town was a big event. Townspeople gathered around the peddler's cart to see all the new things they might buy.

Yankee peddlers were famous for selling a spice called nutmeg, which was hard to obtain in the colonies. It was popular with colonists, who used it to season pies and bread. A nutmeg looks like a gnarly, wooden ball or a walnut. Some Connecticut peddlers sold fake wooden nutmegs to the colonists. By the time the colonists realized they had been swindled, the peddlers were long gone. Yankee peddlers became so well known for selling fake nutmegs that people began to refer to Connecticut as the "Nutmeg State."

Connecticut Yankees were known for being self-sufficient. They grew or made almost everything they needed. They valued their freedom and had a good life overall. After the French and Indian War, the people of the

Land of Steady Habits settled back into a slow, but prosperous existence. They would soon face a time when solid habits would not be enough. They would have to take action to preserve their way of life.

Connecticut's Yale College

John Davenport, the founder of New Haven, had planned to start a college there. But his school was never built. Instead, college students from Connecticut attended Harvard University near Boston.

Then, in 1701, ten Connecticut ministers met to discuss building a college of their own. At the meeting, each minister donated some books to start a college library. Then they sent a petition to the Connecticut General Assembly, which approved the project. The result was Yale College, the third-oldest college in the United States. Only Harvard, established in 1636, and the College of William and Mary, established in 1693 in Williamsburg, Virginia, are older.

Yale opened its doors in 1702, in the town of Bradford, under the name of the Collegiate School. Classes were held in the home of a minister, who had just one student. When a rich merchant named Elihu Yale donated money to the school in 1716, it was renamed Yale College and moved to New Haven. Today it is one of the nation's top universities.

CHAPTER SIX
The Coming Storm

The Stamp Act

During the French and Indian War, Connecticut merchants earned a great deal of money. The British government bought food, ammunition, and other supplies for its troops from Connecticut businesses. When the war ended in 1763, with the American continent firmly in the hands of the English, many businesses fell on hard times. Soldiers returning from the war could not find jobs. And Connecticut was not alone. All of the colonies suffered from an economic **depression** after the war.

The British government decided that the colonies should pay some of the war's costs. The government decided to tax the colonies to raise money. This was the first time that the British had imposed a tax on the colonists. They expected that the colonies would accept the tax without question. The British could not have been more wrong.

Colonists burned papers with government stamps on them in protest against the British Parliament's Stamp Act.

In 1765, the British **Parliament** passed the Stamp Act. This was a tax on all paper goods sold in the colonies. Paper items such as legal documents, newspapers, playing cards, licenses, and pamphlets all had to have an official government stamp before they could be sold. The stamps were similar to postage stamps. Whoever sold the items had to pay the British government a tax to get the stamp.

The colonists in Connecticut and throughout the thirteen colonies were outraged. They vowed to fight against the stamp taxes. They formed anti-tax groups and protested in the streets. A secret society called the Sons of Liberty led attacks on British officials selling stamps. The Sons of Liberty was made up of merchants and tradesmen who fought the new taxes. The *Connecticut Courant* of January 13, 1766, reported a statement from members of the Sons of Liberty:

That we will oppose the same [Stamp Act]
to the last extremity, even to take the field [fight].

It was not long before they kept their word and attacked a British tax collector. The stamp master (tax collector) for Connecticut was a man named Jared Ingersoll. He was a respected business leader who had volunteered to become the stamp master. He thought the Stamp Act was a fair way for the British to tax its colonial citizens. Many people in

Connecticut violently disagreed with him. In the town of Lebanon, colonists made a stuffed dummy of Ingersoll, dragged it through the streets, and burned it. He became so unpopular that the townspeople of New Haven finally voted to replace him as stamp master.

Ingersoll decided to appeal to the governor for help. He set off on horseback for Hartford, the state capital. As he rode along, between 500 and 1,000 men, mostly Sons of Liberty, fell in behind him. Carrying clubs and sticks, the crowd demanded that he sign a letter of resignation and deliver it to the governor in Hartford. After several hours, Ingersoll gave in. When he reached Hartford, he read his resignation before the cheering crowd.

Colonists protesting the Stamp Act confronted the British tax collector on his journey to Hartford and demanded his resignation.

Similar protests occurred throughout the thirteen colonies. When word of these protests reached British lawmakers, they sent soldiers to control the rebellious colonists. Clashes between the soldiers and the colonists broke out regularly.

The British Parliament soon realized that the Stamp Act had been a mistake and repealed it within a year. When news of the repeal reached Connecticut, people celebrated in the streets. The feeling of victory would not last, but the colonists had learned that they could stand up to the British if they stuck together.

Stamp Act Fireworks

When the Stamp Act was repealed in March 1766, people throughout the colonies rejoiced. When the news reached Connecticut, May 23 was declared an official holiday to celebrate. In Hartford, twenty-one cannons were fired and there was a great fireworks display that evening. Unfortunately, a school building that was being used to store gun powder blew up, killing six men.

East vs. West

Not every colonist in Connecticut and the other colonies agreed with the Stamp Act protests. Many colonists remained loyal to the British government and did not want to defy its wishes. Those who supported British policies were called Loyalists or Tories. Those who opposed the British called themselves Patriots. In Connecticut, Loyalists and Patriots split the state into two camps.

The Connecticut River ran down the middle of the colony. Colonists who lived east of the river were mostly Patriots. They were mainly farmers and tradesmen who lived in and around small towns. These colonists were used to running their own affairs and did not like the British telling them what to do.

Western Connecticut contained the colony's major towns, including Hartford and New Haven. This part of the colony was dominated by wealthy farmers and business owners. Most of them wanted peaceful relations with the British and opposed actions like the Stamp Act protests. These Loyalists did not like paying taxes, but they did not want to fight with the British authorities either. They felt that the British Parliament was the supreme authority over the colonists and that they should obey its laws.

The division between eastern and western Connecticut was the main issue in the election of 1766. The Sons of Liberty wanted a new governor. They opposed the current governor, Thomas Fitch. He was from western Connecticut, and a supporter of the British. They campaigned for William Pitkin for governor and Jonathan Trumbull for deputy governor.

The easterners won the election and took over the Connecticut assembly and the governorship. This made Connecticut the only colony with a governor and assembly that were in many ways anti-British. Governor Pitkin died in office in 1769, and Trumbull took over. He remained the governor of Connecticut until 1784 and was a leading Patriot during the Revolutionary War.

Patriots vs. Tories

The Patriots, especially the Sons of Liberty, were known for treating Loyalists very badly. As the Revolution grew closer, acts of violence against Tories happened more and more often.

One particularly cruel act against Loyalists was tarring and feathering. Tories, and sometimes suspected Tories, were covered in hot tar and then coated with feathers. If the Loyalists were lucky, this was done with their clothes on. But often they were first stripped and then covered with the hot tar.

As war grew closer, acts of violence such as nailing a Tory's coat to a post increased.

Some Patriots even scalped Loyalists. Portions of their hair and scalp were cut off with a knife and displayed in the town square. This was a warning to other Tories to leave town. Many did.

More Taxes

When the Stamp Act was repealed, the British government did not give up its idea of taxing the colonies. The British still needed money to pay for the French and Indian War and to support their troops in America. They were determined to have the colonies pay their share. The British Parliament tried twice more to tax the colonies. These new attempts at collecting taxes turned the colonists against the British even more.

First the British tried taxing certain items, including paint, paper, glass, lead, and tea. These were all goods that were not made in the colonies and had to be imported from England. The taxes were called the Townshend Acts. They were named after the head of the British treasury, who had created the new taxes.

Just as before, the colonists protested. This time they refused to buy British goods of any sort. Instead, they made do with what they could make themselves or **smuggle** into the colonies from other countries like Holland, France, and Spain. British merchants lost money when the colonists did not buy their goods.

The city of Boston, Massachusetts, became the center for protest against the Townshend Acts. As a result, the British sent extra troops into the city to control the crowd. On March 5, 1770, a mob of protesters threw stones at a group of British soldiers. The soldiers fired their muskets into the crowd and killed five people. As news of the Boston Massacre spread, Patriots throughout the colonies became outraged. The Boston Massacre and other protests by the colonists convinced the British to repeal the Townshend Acts. It was clear to everyone that the Patriots were growing bolder in their challenges of the British government.

The Boston Tea Party

Even though the Stamp Act and the Townshend Acts failed, the British Parliament was still determined to raise money from the colonies. In 1773, it passed a new law called the Tea Act. The Tea Act was not a tax. It allowed British companies to sell their tea at lower prices than other companies. The British government got money from these companies but it did not get money from others selling tea.

British lawmakers hoped the colonists would be happy about this act since it meant lower prices for tea. But the colonists saw the Tea Act as another attempt by the British to control their lives. Thousands of colonists refused to buy British tea. Instead, Patriot women made "Liberty Tea" for their families from sassafras bark or raspberry leaves.

Patriots in several colonies destroyed shipments of tea as they arrived so they could not be sold. The most famous of these incidents was called the Boston Tea Party. A group of

Patriots dressed as Indians threw a shipment of British tea into Boston Harbor. The British demanded that the colonists pay for the tea. When they refused, British officials closed down Boston's port. No ships were allowed in or out of Boston Harbor. This meant that Boston was cut off from supplies of food and other goods. With the harbor closed, many merchants went out of business. People lost their jobs, and soon Boston ran short of food. Thousands of Bostonians were in danger of starving.

The Boston Tea Party is the most famous of the colonists' protests against the Tea Act, which was passed by the British Parliament.

When word of this crisis spread, the other colonies united in support of the people of Boston. They smuggled food and other supplies into the city. Colonists in Connecticut sent corn, beef, fish, and sugar. The Boston Patriot Samuel Adams wrote that "an attack upon the liberties of one Colony is an attack upon the liberties of us all." Many colonists, including those in Connecticut, agreed with Adams's words.

The Colonists Take Action

Colonial leaders decided to work together to solve their problems with England. In 1774, representatives from twelve of the thirteen colonies met in Philadelphia, Pennsylvania, to decide what to do. (The colony of Georgia did not send anyone to the meeting.) The meeting was called the First Continental Congress. The Connecticut Assembly sent three of its leading citizens, Roger Sherman, Eliphalet Dyer, and Silas Deane.

The meeting of the First Continental Congress took place at Carpenter's Hall in Philadelphia, Pennsylvania.

Most of the representatives at the First Continental Congress still hoped for a peaceful solution to the conflicts with England. But while they hoped for the best, they also prepared for the worst. The colonial leaders directed the colonies to prepare militias in case of war with England. In Connecticut, towns began assembling their militia forces and stocking up on military supplies. Many Loyalists were forced to leave the state as the Sons of Liberty and other Patriots prepared for war.

CHAPTER SEVEN

War and Revolution

War Begins

After the First Continental Congress, every colony, including Connecticut, began gathering weapons and training its militia. Patriot leaders like Samuel Adams and John Hancock openly urged the colonists to resist Britain's rule. The British were not happy that the colonists were preparing for war.

On April 19, 1775, the British commander in Boston sent troops to Lexington, Massachusetts, to arrest Adams and Hancock. When the British arrived, a group of Massachusetts militiamen confronted them on the town green. The militiamen were outnumbered and outgunned. Even though Adams and Hancock escaped, eight militiamen were killed and ten more were wounded.

The British quickly decided to march to the nearby town of Concord to destroy **stockpiles** of Patriot military supplies. Word spread quickly among the Massachusetts farmers and

Colonial militiamen were outnumbered by British soldiers in Lexington, Massachusetts, in the first battle of the Revolutionary War.

tradesmen who had been preparing for war. Hundreds of militiamen gathered near the North Bridge leading into Concord. This time, the Patriots outnumbered the British.

The British soldiers marched up the road in neat rows and began to cross the bridge. Patriots hiding behind trees, fences, and rocks began shooting and killing the soldiers. The British soldiers fired back and then began to retreat. But the Patriots kept shooting until nearly 300 British soldiers were killed. The Patriots had won their first battle in what was to be a long and deadly war.

Connecticut Responds

Word of the battles at Lexington and Concord spread quickly to Connecticut. A post rider named Israel Bissell rode his horse so hard that the animal collapsed and died. Within three days, every town had heard the news.

A student named Ebenezer Fitch at Yale College in New Haven wrote in his diary:

> *"Friday, April 21. To-day tidings of the battle of Lexington, which is the first engagement with the British troops, arrived at New Haven. This filled the country with alarm, and rendered it impossible for us to pursue our studies to any profit."*

Nearly 4,000 farmers, merchants, tradesmen, and fishermen stopped what they were doing and sprang into action. Grabbing their muskets, they said good-bye to their families and marched toward Cambridge, Massachusetts, to join the American troops gathering there. The Connecticut militia was led by General Israel Putnam, a founder of the Sons of Liberty. When they arrived in Cambridge, Putnam and his Connecticut militiamen prepared to face the British in the first major battle of the Revolution.

American troops waited atop Breed's Hill, in a temporary fort built of dirt and rocks, near Boston. Meanwhile, the British mounted cannons on nearby Bunker Hill. On June 17, 1775, the British charged up Breed's Hill and were met by a hail of bullets from the Americans' muskets and cannons. Hundreds of English soldiers fell, and the British retreated. But they soon charged again. Once more, they fell back under heavy American fire.

When the British charged a third time, the Americans were almost out of ammunition. General Putnam galloped on his horse behind his troops, urging them not to give up. He then shouted the famous words, "Don't fire until you see the whites of their eyes." In the end, however, the Patriots were forced to abandon the hill to the British.

When the battle was over, the British had lost more than 1,000 soldiers. The Americans lost almost 400. Although they did not win, the Americans considered the Battle of Bunker Hill a great victory. They had shown the British that American soldiers could fight bravely. News of the battle spread and brought hope to colonial militiamen. The colonists started to believe that they actually could fight against, and even beat, trained British soldiers.

The Second Continental Congress

The Second Continental Congress opened in Philadelphia in July 1775, just three weeks after the battles at Lexington and Concord. Some **delegates** still hoped that the colonies could peacefully settle their differences with England.

In August, King George III of England issued a proclamation declaring that the **rebellion** in the colonies would be put down by force. At the same time, he sent more troops to America. By the following spring, most of the delegates at the Second Continental Congress agreed that there was no way to patch things up with England. They felt that the thirteen colonies should break away from England and become an independent country. This meant that the colonies would have to fight the British for their freedom, but they were willing to take the chance.

Independence

On July 2, 1776, delegates to the Second Continental Congress took a historic poll. On that day, twelve colonies voted to make themselves independent states. New York did not vote at first, but cast its vote with the others a few days later. The colonies now were no longer part of England. They were now joined together as the United States of America.

Thomas Jefferson, a representative from Virginia, wrote the Declaration of Independence at the request of the Second Continental Congress.

The members of the Second Continental Congress had asked Thomas Jefferson, one of the representatives from Virginia, to write a document to explain why the colonies wanted to take such drastic action. On July 4, 1776, the Continental Congress voted to approve Jefferson's Declaration of Independence. In August, the representatives signed the declaration, making it their official statement to the world. Every person who signed knew that if the colonies lost the war, the signers were all likely to be hanged as traitors by the English. Four men from Connecticut put their signatures on the Declaration of Independence. They were Roger Sherman, Samuel Huntington, William Williams, and Oliver Wolcott.

Connecticut Cannons

At the beginning of the American Revolution, the Patriots desperately needed cannons. They knew they could not win against the British without cannons to arm their ships and defend their forts. The Patriot army turned to the iron and cannon foundry in Salisbury, Connecticut. It was the most important cannon factory in New England.

During the war, Salisbury cast more than 800 cannons, plus cannon balls and grenades, for the Patriot cause. Without these cannons, Patriot ships would have lost many battles. Forts would not have been able to defend themselves. The Salisbury cannon works was Connecticut's most important wartime industry.

Fighting the War

England did not give up its colonies without a fight. It was determined to use its powerful army and navy to hold onto the American colonies. The British sent thousands of troops to America to fight the colonists, whom they called "rebels." The British troops occupied America's largest cities of New York, Philadelphia, Boston, and Charles Town, South Carolina. They blocked shipments of supplies and food from reaching the Americans, and they arrested and hanged many Patriots.

The war lasted for eight years and cost the new nation thousands of lives. Against the might of the British army and navy, the United States had only a small band of soldiers from the colonial militias. These were combined into the Continental army under the leadership of General George Washington.

Most of the Continentals were not trained soldiers. They were farmers and tradesmen who joined the army to fight for a cause they believed worthy. Every colony sent soldiers to fight for the new nation. Connecticut sent almost 40,000 troops, out of a population of 200,000 people. It contributed more troops to the war effort than any state except Massachusetts.

When British soldiers launched their second attack in the town of Greenwich, the Connecticut militia won the battle and saved the town.

The War in Connecticut

The citizens of Connecticut were very lucky during the war. The fighting destroyed many towns and cities in other states. British troops did invade Connecticut four times during the war. But only a few towns were attacked, and there were no major losses of life.

The first British raid on Connecticut happened in April 1777. Two thousand British troops landed at Compo Beach on Long Island Sound. Then they marched about 20 miles (32 kilometers) north to the town of Danbury. The soldiers burned down nineteen houses and destroyed thousands of barrels of pork, beef, and flour. In addition, they burned 5,000 pairs of shoes, 2,000 bushels (70,000 liters) of grain, and 1,600 tents. As the British were leaving the area, they were attacked by American militiamen.

The battle was small but the impact on the Continental army was large. The tents, food, and other supplies lost at Danbury were almost irreplaceable. As a result of this raid, General Washington ordered all supplies moved farther away from the coast to prevent similar losses in the future.

In February 1779, British troops launched their second attack. The town of Greenwich, on Connecticut's southwestern tip, was the target. This time, the Connecticut militia was prepared. It drove the British back, saving the town. The third British strike on Connecticut took place in July 1779, as British troops battled their way into New Haven. After killing and wounding several people there, they traveled to the town of Fairfield, where they destroyed about 200 homes and other buildings. The third attack finally ended in nearby Norwalk, where the British burned down most of the houses.

Connecticut's Traitor

The most famous traitor of the Revolutionary War and perhaps the most famous in American history was born in Norwich, Connecticut. His name was Benedict Arnold. Arnold joined the Continental army at the beginning of the Revolution in 1775. He fought bravely during the battles at Fort Ticonderoga and Saratoga in New York. George Washington praised him and made him commander of the Continental army in Philadelphia. Arnold was an American hero.

In Philadelphia, Arnold went to many parties and gambled. Soon he owed money to many Loyalists living in the city.

The British offered Arnold money to pay his debts if he gave American army secrets to them. Arnold accepted the offer, but the Americans soon discovered his treason.

Arnold escaped to the British army and became an officer. He fought against his former friends, even taking part in a raid on his home colony of Connecticut. After the war, Arnold moved to England, where he died in 1801. In the end, Arnold received less than one-third of the money he had been promised by the British. In America, the name Benedict Arnold became a synonym for the word *traitor*.

The fourth, final, and most serious British raid in Connecticut took place in 1781. It was led by Benedict Arnold, an American general and hero who had turned against the Americans and joined the British forces. On September 6, Arnold and about 2,000 British soldiers marched on the towns of New London and Groton. The British troops destroyed large parts of New London and attacked Fort Griswold, which protected the town of Groton. The Americans fought bravely, but were greatly outnumbered and forced to surrender the fort. As the American commander handed over his sword, he was killed by a British soldier. The British then opened fire on the other Americans, killing about eighty militiamen.

The massacre happened only a few miles from Benedict Arnold's boyhood home. Arnold was blamed for the murders of the Connecticut militiamen, even though he was not at Fort Griswold when they were killed.

Connecticut's Navy

Connecticut's location on Long Island Sound meant that its citizens owned many ships. The ships were used for fishing and for transporting goods. When the war broke out, the captains of Connecticut's ships wanted to help the Patriot cause. Connecticut's sea captains managed to capture more than forty British ships during the war. The cargo from these ships was used to support the Continental army.

Some Connecticut coastal towns became bases for privateers. Privateers were pirates and other ship captains who were employed by countries such as the United States to fight their enemies. The Continental navy had only a few ships, so the Americans hired privateers to attack the British vessels carrying food and supplies to their troops. The privateers formed an unofficial navy. Privateers from all the colonies captured over 500 British supply ships and turned over the cargo to the Continental army.

Coastal towns in Connecticut became bases for colonists' ships that were turned over to the military to fight the British in Long Island Sound.

Black Soldiers

Many Connecticut slaves and free black people served in the Continental army and navy during the Revolutionary War. Many slaves were eager to fight for the American cause. They thought that they might be freed after the war.

In Connecticut, many white citizens were opposed to slavery by the beginning of the Revolution. They were more willing than southern slave masters to free slaves who fought for the Americans during the war. A few slaves fought in the first battles of the Revolution at Lexington and Concord. Others joined the Continental army as the war dragged on. The slaves fought on the front lines alongside white soldiers and sailors in integrated units. Many died for the American cause. After the war, Connecticut abolished slavery within the state through the Gradual Emancipation Acts beginning in 1784.

On the other side, the British guaranteed that any slave who fought for *them* would be freed. Many slaves from the southern colonies joined the British side.

The War Ends

After eight years of fighting, the Americans finally achieved victory. The end came when the commander of the British army, Charles Cornwallis, fell into a trap. He led 7,000 British troops to a village called Yorktown on the Virginia coast. The British thought they would meet ships there carrying supplies. Instead, a fleet of French warships had come to help the Patriots win the war. The French ships trapped the English fleet in Chesapeake Bay a few miles north of Yorktown.

Instead of supply ships, Cornwallis faced the cannons of the French navy when he arrived at Yorktown. At the same time, 8,000 American troops and 8,000 French troops cut off any hope of a British escape by land.

A great battle raged back and forth for weeks. Finally, Cornwallis realized that he was running out of supplies, including gunpowder and ammunition. He surrendered to Washington on October 17, 1781. This was the last major battle in the war. Within a year, the British troops left America.

General Cornwallis surrendered to George Washington after the battle at Yorktown, when British supplies were depleted and all routes for escape had been blocked by the colonial army.

After the War

After the war, the thirteen colonies still faced many challenges. Farms, towns, and businesses had been damaged by eight years of fighting. The British had stopped many ships from bringing goods to American ports. This made everyday items, like sugar or shoes, both scarce and expensive. Paper money had little value. Most manufactured goods were too expensive for the average family.

Connecticut had one great advantage over some other states following the war. The people trusted Governor Trumbull and the other members of the state government. Almost everyone who remained in the state after the war had been a Patriot. They had elected Trumbull before the war, and they still trusted him at the end of the war. Other states, which had British governors before the war, had to struggle to set up their new state governments. Connecticut continued with the same laws that it used before and during the war.

Throughout its history, Connecticut's citizens had always been independent. Now the new state had to learn how to be a part of a much larger country. The people would have to find a balance between their independent nature and the need for a unified government for all thirteen states.

CHAPTER EIGHT

A New Government

The Constitutional Convention

Connecticut's state government was working well after the Revolutionary War. But the government of the whole country was having serious problems. During the war, the United States was governed by a set of laws called the Articles of Confederation. These laws had been created during the Second Continental Congress. But when the war was over, the Articles of Confederation were not enough to hold the country together.

There was no president under the Articles of Confederation. There were no national courts and no national money system. The United States government had no way of raising money because it could not tax its citizens. Overall, the individual states had much more power than the federal (central) government. In addition, most people at the time felt more loyalty to their state than to the United States.

◁ *This political cartoon from 1787 shows the Constitution as a wagon stuck in the mud being pulled in two directions.*

Many of America's leaders knew that the United States needed a stronger form of government. They believed a strong federal government would gain the respect of other countries. Also, a strong government would ensure the unity of the thirteen states.

Other leaders worried that if the federal government was too strong, it would take away the rights of the states and the individual citizens. These leaders did not want to return to a government like the one they had struggled against under British rule. Everyone agreed that something had to be done quickly.

The leaders of the thirteen states decided to hold a meeting to strengthen the Articles of Confederation. Connecticut sent three of its leading citizens to represent the state. They were Oliver Ellsworth, William Samuel Johnson, and Roger Sherman.

Soon the delegates realized that the Articles of Confederation would not be enough to govern the country even if they were changed. They needed a new set of laws. They decided to write an entirely new constitution. The meeting became known as the Constitutional Convention.

Roger Sherman was one of Connecticut's delegates to the Constitutional Convention.

The Connecticut Compromise

Not everyone agreed on the wording for the new constitution. It had to balance the rights of individuals and the states with those of the federal government. Otherwise, it would not be accepted by all the states or all the citizens.

The delegates **debated** for more than four months. One of the biggest conflicts was over the number of lawmakers each state would have in the federal government. This was important because each lawmaker would get one vote. The states with the most citizens thought that the number should be determined by population. Smaller states objected that this arrangement would give the large states too much power. The smaller states wanted each state to have the same number of lawmakers. The debate went on and on.

Then, Roger Sherman proposed a compromise. He suggested that there should be two lawmaking bodies in the federal government. They would be called the House of Representatives and the Senate. Each state would elect members of the House of Representatives based on the population of the state. Larger states would have more representatives than smaller states. In the Senate, each state would have the same number of representatives. At first this number was set at one, but then it was changed to two senators from each state. That made the states equal in the Senate no matter what their population.

Sherman's proposal was called the Connecticut Compromise. It was quickly accepted by both large and small states. The system of two lawmaking bodies is still the basis for the legislative branch of the U.S. government today.

Without the Connecticut Compromise, all thirteen states would not have signed the Constitution.

Counting Slaves

Once the states agreed to the Connecticut Compromise, there was one other difficult issue to resolve. The states had to decide how to count their slaves in the population. States with large slave populations would have more members in the House of Representatives if slaves were counted. Those states would therefore have more power. Counting slaves was especially important for states like South Carolina, where more than half the population were slaves.

This issue was a difficult one for many delegates to the Constitutional Convention for several reasons. First, it seemed unfair to count slaves in order to give a state's white population more members in the House. Slaves could not vote and had no rights. Second, many people, especially in the North, believed that slavery was wrong and wanted to end it in the United States. Counting slaves would make that goal more difficult.

The southern slave states were determined not to agree to the new constitution unless slaves were counted in some way. In the end, the states reached another compromise. Three-fifths of the slave population would be counted. This meant that every five slaves counted as three free people in the state's population.

Freeing Connecticut's Slaves

The issue of slavery would continue to divide the states in the North from those in the South for another eighty years. Slavery was gradually abolished in Connecticut by new state laws. They were called the Gradual Emancipation Acts of 1784 and 1797. These laws freed slaves over time. The act of 1784 stated that all slaves born after 1784 would become free at the age of twenty-five. The act of 1797 changed the age to twenty-one. By 1800, more than 80 percent of Connecticut's black citizens were free. By 1848, thirteen years before the Civil War began, there were only six slaves in Connecticut.

Approving the Constitution

The U.S. Constitution was completed in September 1787. In January 1788, delegates from each town in Connecticut met in Hartford to decide whether or not to approve the Constitution. The town delegates talked and argued for five days. Finally, on January 9, Connecticut delegates approved the Constitution by a vote of 128 to 40. Connecticut was the fifth state to approve the new U.S. Constitution.

In less than 200 years, Connecticut had grown from a wilderness to a vital part of the new country. It had always been a place where independent people could find freedom and opportunity. As the new nation grew, the state of Connecticut would continue to make important contributions to the United States.

Connecticut families enjoyed the benefits of living in their new state. Their hard work allowed many of them to live in comfortable homes.

Recipe

Pease Porridge

Many people think of porridge as a hot breakfast cereal similar to oatmeal. In the American colonies, it was a thick soup. Farmers would sometimes put a bowl of porridge with a string in it outside on the porch on a cold winter night. The porridge would freeze solid. The next day, they would carry the frozen porridge into the field and hang it from a tree by the string. When lunchtime came, they would start a fire, take the porridge down from the tree, and heat it in a pot.

Pease porridge was a popular dish. The word *pease* was an old form of the word *pea*. It was so popular there was a children's rhyme about it.

Pease porridge hot,
Pease porridge cold,
Pease porridge in the pot,
Nine days old.

Modern Version

This colonial recipe for pease porridge serves eight—frozen or thawed.

2 cups dried split peas
2 1/2 quarts cold water
2 teaspoons salt
2 stalks celery
2 medium onions
2 teaspoons dried mint or 4 teaspoons chopped, fresh mint leaves

- Rinse the peas and soak them overnight in 2 1/2 quarts cold water.
- Add salt to the water and peas.
- Bring the water with the peas to a boil.
- Reduce the heat and simmer the peas in the water for about 3 hours.
- Chop the celery, onions, and mint and add to the peas and water.
- Simmer for another 30 minutes.

This activity should be done with adult supervision.

Activity

Hornbook

A hornbook was one of the first books used by children in colonial times. Hornbooks were made from slabs of wood shaped like paddles. A piece of paper with printing or writing was attached to the paddle.

The name *hornbook* came from the piece of cow's horn that covered the paper. The horn was cut into a very thin sheet and placed over the paper to protect it from damage. The cow horn was so thin, children could see right through it.

Alphabet letters, numbers, or prayers were often written on the different pages placed under the cow horn. The handle of most hornbooks had a hole at its end with rope threaded through it. Children often wore their hornbooks around their necks or attached them to their belts using the rope.

Directions

You can make a hornbook.

*Heavy cardboard • Pencil • Scissors
Glue or paste • Blank paper
Wax paper or cellophane*

- Draw a large paddle shape on the cardboard. Cut out the paddle.
- Trace the paddle, minus its handle, on the blank sheet of paper.
- Cut out this shape.
- Write a lesson for a young student on the paper. You can write upper- and lowercase letters or numbers. You can draw pictures of animals and label them with their names.
- Paste this sheet onto the paddle.
- Cut out a piece of wax paper or cellophane slightly larger than the hornbook.
- Place the cellophane over the paper that contains the lesson. Fold it over the cardboard and tape on back.

This activity should be done with adult supervision.

CONNECTICUT
Time Line

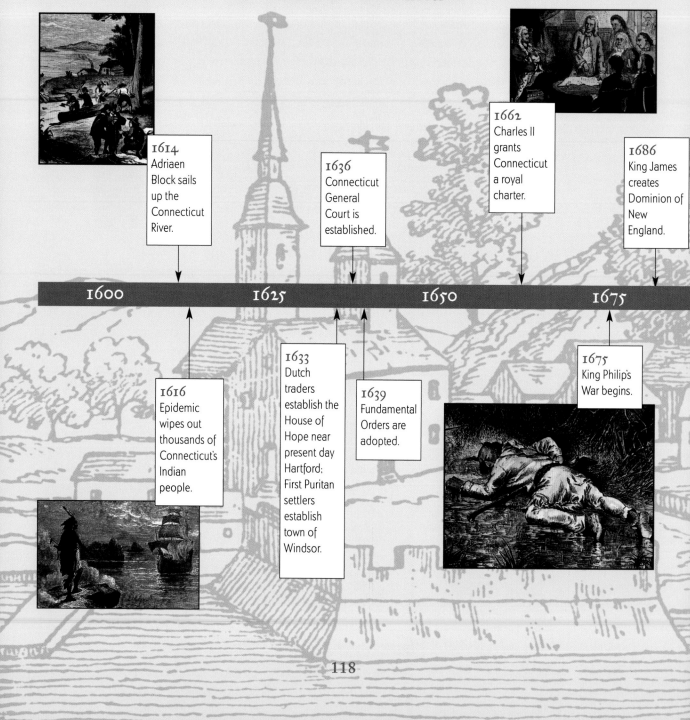

1614
Adriaen Block sails up the Connecticut River.

1636
Connecticut General Court is established.

1662
Charles II grants Connecticut a royal charter.

1686
King James creates Dominion of New England.

1600   **1625**   **1650**   **1675**

1616
Epidemic wipes out thousands of Connecticut's Indian people.

1633
Dutch traders establish the House of Hope near present day Hartford; First Puritan settlers establish town of Windsor.

1639
Fundamental Orders are adopted.

1675
King Philip's War begins.

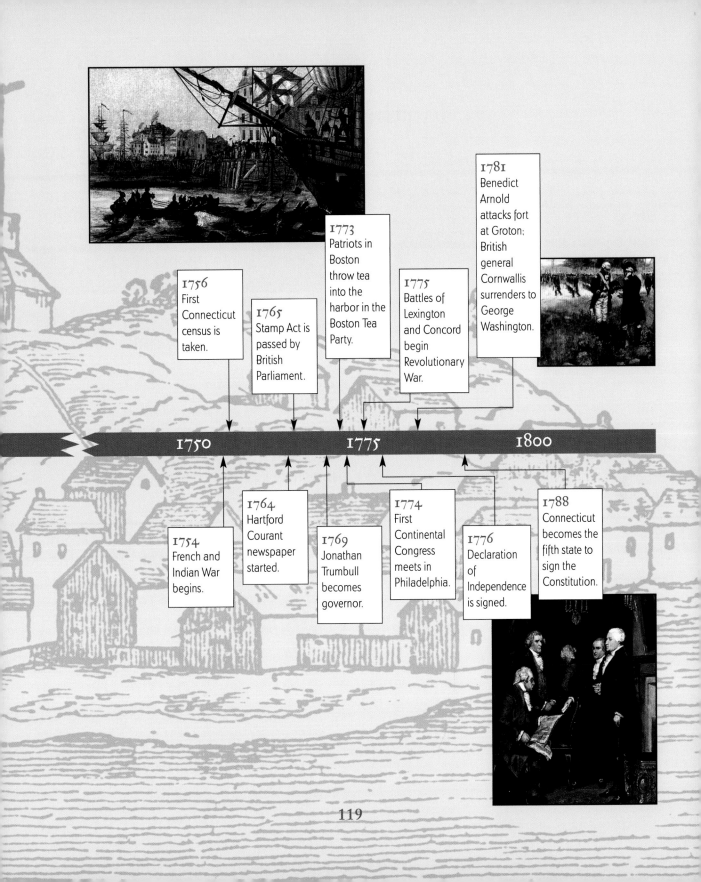

1756
First Connecticut census is taken.

1765
Stamp Act is passed by British Parliament.

1773
Patriots in Boston throw tea into the harbor in the Boston Tea Party.

1775
Battles of Lexington and Concord begin Revolutionary War.

1781
Benedict Arnold attacks fort at Groton; British general Cornwallis surrenders to George Washington.

1750   **1775**   **1800**

1754
French and Indian War begins.

1764
Hartford Courant newspaper started.

1769
Jonathan Trumbull becomes governor.

1774
First Continental Congress meets in Philadelphia.

1776
Declaration of Independence is signed.

1788
Connecticut becomes the fifth state to sign the Constitution.

119

Further Reading

Abate, Frank. *Connecticut Trivia.* Nashville, TN: Rutledge Hill Press, 2001.

Johnson, Claudia Durst. *Daily Life in Colonial New England.* Westport, CT: Greenwood Press, 2002.

Perl, Lila. *Sumps, Grunts, and Snickerdoodles: What Colonial America Ate and Why.* New York, NY: Seabury Press, 1975.

Philips, David E. *Legendary Connecticut: Traditional Tales from the Nutmeg State.* Willimantic, CT: Curbstone Press, 1992.

Purvis, Thomas L. *Almanacs of American Life: Colonial America to 1763.* New York, NY: Facts on File, 1999.

Taylor, Dale. *The Writer's Guide to Everyday Life in Colonial America.* Cincinnati, OH: Writer's Digest Books, 1997.

Glossary

alliance a close association between nations to protect their common interests

allies people united with others for a common purpose

census an official count of the citizens of a state or country

clapboard a long narrow board used to cover the side of a house

constitution the basic system of laws of a country

corrupt doing wrong or behaving in a bad or improper way

debate to discuss opposing points of view

delegate someone who is appointed or elected to represent others

democratic believing or practicing the idea that people are equal

depression a period of economic decline or hard times

diphtheria a deadly disease that causes difficulty breathing

fertile producing large crops

intolerant unwilling to accept differences in beliefs

migrate to move from one country or region to another

militia an army made up of ordinary citizens rather than professional soldiers

mobile easily moved

palisade a fence made of poles to protect against attack

Parliament the group of people who make the laws in England

rebellion an armed resistance to the established government

repeal to cancel or take back an official act or law

representative a person who speaks for others at a meeting

smallpox a disease that causes large, pus-filled pimples, high fever, and often death

smuggle to take something in or out of a country illegally, especially to avoid taxes

sound a long, narrow body of water, wider than a strait, that connects two other bodies of water

stockade a line of strong stakes driven into the ground and set up as a defense

stockpile a supply stored for future use

stronghold a fortress or protected fort

treaty an agreement between two or more countries

Index